SPOTLIGHT ON SOCIAL AND EMOTIONAL LEARNING

KNOW WHO YOU ARE

ACCURATE SELF-PERCEPTION

MARIEL BARD

PowerKiDS press™

NEW YORK

Published in 2020 by The Rosen Publishing Group, Inc.
29 East 21st Street, New York, NY 10010

Editor: Rachel Gintner
Designer: Michael Flynn

Photo Credits: Cover Steve Debenport/E+/Getty Images; cover, pp. 1, 3–4, 6, 8, 10–14, 16, 18–20, 22–24 (background) TairA/Shutterstock.com; pp. 5, 13, 19 Monkey Business Images/Shutterstock.com; p. 6 A. RICARDO/ Shutterstock.com; p. 7 https://commons.wikimedia.org/wiki/File:ADELE_LIVE_2017_at_ADELAIDE_OVAL_-_Sweet_ Devotion.jpg; p. 9 (main) Fotokostic/Shutterstock.com; p. 9 (inset) Alfa Photostudio/Shutterstock.com; p. 10 Arman Novic/Shutterstock.com; p. 11 chuabanral ekawat/Shutterstock.com; p. 12 Syda Productions/Shutterstock.com; p. 15 Jamie Squire/Getty Images; p. 16 Gavran333/Shutterstock.com; p. 17 courtesy of the Library of Congress; p. 18 Roman Samborskyi/Shutterstock.com; p. 21 KidStock/Blend Images/Getty Images; p. 22 OG175/Shutterstock.com.

Cataloging-in-Publication Data

Names: Bard, Mariel.
Title: Know who you are: accurate self-perception / Mariel Bard.
Description: New York : PowerKids Press, 2020. | Series: Spotlight on social and emotional learning | Includes glossary and index.
Identifiers: ISBN 9781725302075 (pbk.) | ISBN 9781725302266 (library bound) | ISBN 9781725302174 (6pack)
Subjects: LCSH: Self-perception in adolescence--Juvenile literature. | Self-perception--Juvenile literature. | Self-acceptance--Juvenile literature. | Self-esteem--Juvenile literature.
Classification: LCC BF697.5.S43 B36 2020 | DDC 155.2--dc23

Manufactured in the United States of America

CPSIA Compliance Information: Batch #CSPK19. For further information contact Rosen Publishing, New York, New York at 1-800-237-9932.

CONTENTS

CHAPTER ONE

WHO AM I?

Think about your friends and family members. What qualities do they have? Are your friends smart? Are your family members caring? We often create perceptions, or understandings, of people in our lives and they create perceptions of us. We also create perceptions of ourselves. You might have an idea in your head of what you're like, and this is called self-perception. The thoughts we have about ourselves affect how we interact with others and how we experience everyday life.

Consider this—have you ever been told by a classmate that you're funny? Has a teacher said that you're kind? Sometimes these comments surprise us, and sometimes we already know we have these qualities! What we perceive might be different from what others see in us. Having a balanced view of ourselves can help us better understand who we are and the world around us.

Interacting with your friends, family, and even your neighbors can help you learn about how you perceive yourself and how they perceive you. Why not start tomorrow? Whether you're at the playground or at home, find out what new things you can learn.

CHAPTER TWO

TAKING STOCK

You can start creating balanced self-perception by working on your **self-awareness**. To be self-aware, you need to think thoughtfully and deeply about yourself. Imagine different situations and how you might act in them—focus on how they make you feel. Do you get nervous speaking in front of a crowd because you might mess up? Or do you get excited to meet people and make new friends? Everyone behaves differently. Knowing how you feel, what you like and dislike, and what **motivates** you to do something all factor into self-awareness.

Being self-aware can improve your relationships with friends and family, too. By knowing how you make others feel, you can better understand their perceptions of you. For example, if people always want to talk with you and ask your opinion, they probably think you're a good listener with useful ideas.

BEYONCÉ

Even some famous singers, such as Adele (shown here), Taylor Swift, and Beyoncé, get nervous performing for an audience. But they're aware of their stage fright and have found ways to manage it!

CHAPTER THREE

WHAT AM I GOOD AT?

Identifying your strengths, or what you're good at, is a positive exercise you can do to **develop** your self-perception. It's helpful to write down what you enjoy and activities you're good at, and then think about why these matter to you. If you like dogs, try to dig deeper into why you like them. Are you good at training dogs and teaching them tricks? This could indicate you have a strength for teaching. Or maybe you like to take care of dogs, doing things such as walking and brushing them. This could indicate you have a strength for caring for others.

Strengths are different from interests because interests, such as fishing, can change, but strengths, such as the patience required to be good at fishing, are part of who you are. Once you identify your strengths, you can decide to take part in activities that will **hone** them.

Trying out different activities, such as dance or sports, can help you decide what you like and discover your strengths.

CHAPTER FOUR

WHAT CAN I WORK ON?

People often consider weaknesses to be the opposite of strengths. However, instead of thinking you're weak at something, try considering it an area for improvement. For example, if you've started playing a musical instrument, you know there's a lot to learn. If you enjoy playing and want to get better, you'll need practice.

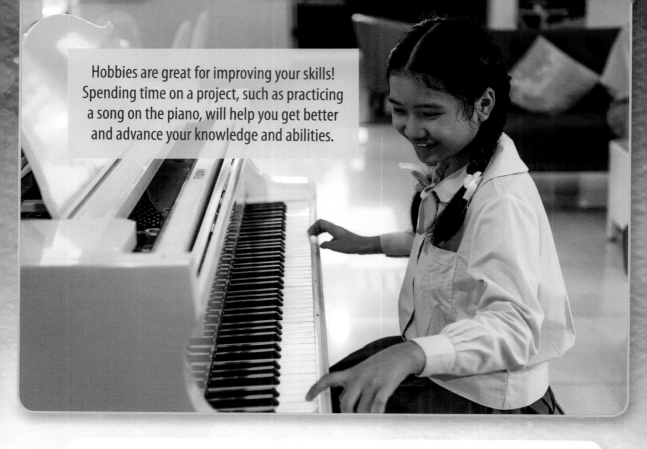

Hobbies are great for improving your skills! Spending time on a project, such as practicing a song on the piano, will help you get better and advance your knowledge and abilities.

Everyone has skills to work on. If one of your interests is baking but your cookies burn, it doesn't mean you're not a good baker. It just means this batch didn't turn out how you wished. Think about where you can improve—maybe you forgot to set a timer, or you misread the instructions. Paying attention, such as carefully following the directions, is a great skill to learn. One bad batch of cookies is only one experience—you will have so many more experiences and more time to try again!

CHAPTER FIVE

CONFIDENCE VERSUS PERCEPTION

Confidence is a feeling of certainty. When you have self-confidence, you feel certain in your abilities. But self-confidence can be tricky because even when you have lots of confidence, you still might fail. For example, imagine you have a test at school. You're confident you know the subject, so you don't study. During the test, you think you've answered everything correctly. But then—surprise!—you find out you didn't do very well. Your confidence overshadowed the fact that you were unprepared.

If you're not feeling confident in a subject or an activity, ask a teacher, a parent, or a friend for assistance. Having support can help you solve problems and build confidence.

In contrast, an exact or balanced self-perception of your abilities allows you to recognize if you really ought to study more or if your confidence is **justified**. While you'll want to avoid being overconfident, a healthy amount of confidence can be beneficial. You'll feel more in control and relaxed, and you'll have that extra boost to tackle tough problems.

CHAPTER SIX

SETTING GOALS

After you've identified your strengths and weaknesses, you might notice a few that you'd like to work on. You can do this by setting goals.

If you have a great imagination, you could have a strength for storytelling. To grow this strength, try setting small goals. For example, read many books to discover what kind of stories you like. Then, organize your ideas—write them down or draw them out—until you decide how the story should go. Soon enough, you'll be telling your own stories!

If you have trouble with a subject, such as spelling, setting goals could help you improve. You could set a **long-term** goal to compete in your school's annual spelling bee. Then, break down your long-term goal into smaller, **short-term** goals. You can start by learning a new word each day, then progress to having your family quiz you at home!

Olympic athlete Jessica Hardy (shown here) focuses on smaller goals, such as eating healthy and completing daily workouts, to help get to her bigger goals. One of her bigger goals is competing in the Olympics.

CHAPTER SEVEN

KEEPING A JOURNAL

Journals are a great way to develop self-perception because they encourage self-reflection. They're a great way to organize your thoughts and keep track of your past perceptions, and you can revisit your journal entries weeks, months, and even years later.

When journaling, try thinking about how you're feeling. What was the best part of your day, and what was the most challenging part? What moods did you experience? To whom did you talk, and how did the conversation make you feel? Keeping track of your actions and **reactions** to different situations allows you to reflect on how each one affects you.

Remember, it doesn't really matter how you write in your journal, because it's just a way for you to show your thoughts and emotions. You can even draw, color, or scribble if you want!

Journaling has been around for centuries. Benjamin Franklin kept many journals, including a collection of his thoughts on how he could improve himself!

CHAPTER EIGHT

ACCEPTING FEEDBACK

If you've ever received a note, such as "excellent job" or "this needs work," from your teacher on a test or assignment, you've received feedback. Feedback is someone else's opinion based on their **unique** view. It's helpful to receive feedback because it lets you know how other people view a situation. Other people's perceptions are often different from your own.

Getting feedback from someone you trust can help you clearly see what your strengths are and where you need to improve.

If you're having an issue you need to work through, it can be helpful to talk to people you trust, such as family, friends, or teachers. These people can give advice or tips on ways to approach the problem. After getting feedback, think about your perception of the issue and why it might be different from their perception. You might get feedback that hurts your feelings—it's never fun to be told you're wrong!—but good feedback should help you learn and improve.

CHAPTER NINE

WHAT DO I BELIEVE AND VALUE?

We believe and value certain things based on our background and experiences. Understanding what you believe and what others around you believe is called social awareness.

You might find that your beliefs and values are similar to those of your friends or family. Sharing common beliefs and values happens because we often have shared experiences with loved ones. For example, if your family values knowledge, you'll probably **prioritize** your education. Or maybe your friends play soccer during their free time because they want to improve their skills. This is a shared belief that practice leads to improvement.

Also, new experiences can change your beliefs and values. Every once in a while, think about what's important to you and why. Look back in your journal—has anything changed? You likely now see yourself and the world differently.

If you want to meet people with shared values, consider joining a club or organization that matches your interests. If you care about a healthy Earth, you could take part in a park cleanup or plant trees.

CHAPTER TEN

THIS IS ME!

Learning about yourself is exciting! Whether you decide to keep a journal or ask others for feedback, your discoveries might surprise you. Or, they might make perfect sense. Either way, when you know your strengths, you can hone them. When you know what you need to work on, you can take steps to improve.

Knowing yourself will help you better understand others. Maybe you share a belief with someone or maybe you understand someone's feelings because you've experienced a similar feeling or situation. While it's important to reflect on yourself, you should also reflect on others and respect them as unique individuals, just as you'd want to be respected.

Think of yourself as a big puzzle you're putting together. When all the pieces of the puzzle fit, you see a complete picture of who you are. And you can step back and say, "This is me!"

GLOSSARY

develop (duh-VEL-uhp) To bring out the possibilities of, to begin to have gradually, or to create over time.

hone (HOHN) To practice something, such as a skill or strength, to get better at that activity.

justify (JUHS-tuh-fy) To show that something is right or deserved.

long-term (LONG–TURM) Lasting or occupying a long period of time.

motivate (MOH-tuh-vayt) To provide with a reason for doing something.

prioritize (pry-OHR-uh-tyz) To list or rate (as in projects or goals) in order of importance.

reaction (ree-ACK-shun) A response to something that happens, such as a change.

self-awareness (SELF–uh-WAYR-nuhs) An awareness of one's own traits or individuality.

short-term (SHORT–TURM) Lasting or occupying a short period of time.

unique (yoo-NEEK) Special or different from anything else.

INDEX

PRIMARY SOURCE LIST

Page 7
Adele performing at Adelaide Oval, Australian tour. Photograph. Rob Sturman. March 13, 2017.

Page 15
U.S. Olympian Jessica Hardy. Photograph. Jamie Squire and Getty Images. June 30, 2012. Getty Images Sport.

Page 17
Benjamin Franklin. Oil painting. Mason Chamberlin. 1762. Philadelphia Museum of Art.

WEBSITES

Due to the changing nature of Internet links, PowerKids Press has developed an online list of websites related to the subject of this book. This site is updated regularly. Please use this link to access the list: www.powerkidslinks.com/SSEL/selfperception